POETS NOW

Edited by Robert Peters

1. *Jonathan Williams*, Get Hot or Get Out
2. *Rochelle Ratner*, Practicing To Be A Woman
3. *Jerry Ratch*, Hot Weather
4. *David Ray*, The Touched Life
5. *Carolyn Stoloff*, A Spool of Blue
6. *Edwin Honig*, Interrupted Praise

HOT WEATHER

Poems Selected and New by Jerry Ratch

Poets Now **3**

The Scarecrow Press, Inc.
Metuchen, N.J., & London   *1982*

BOOKS BY JERRY RATCH

Puppet X, (First Edition), Shameless Hussy Press, 1973
Puppet X, (Second Edition), Shameless Hussy Press, 1976
Clown Birth, Shameless Hussy Press, 1975
The Suburban Poem, Nemesis Press, 1975
Osiris, Cloud Marauder Press, 1977
Chaucer Marginalia, Sombre Reptiles Press, 1979
Rose, Sombre Reptiles Press, 1979
Helen, Cloud Marauder Press, 1982

Library of Congress Cataloging in Publication Data

Ratch, Jerry.
  Hot weather.

  (Poets now   ; no. 3)
  I. Title.   II. Series.
PS3568.A715H66   811'.54   81-21473
ISBN 0-8108-1511-7   AACR2

"rat in the sun
rat in the sun"

INTRODUCTION

Jerry Ratch's formative years as a poet were the sixties, the years of the counterculture revolution, of student uprisings, of mass demonstrations against the Asian wars, of marches on behalf of oppressed blacks and gays. As a young poet, himself scarred by polio, observing and participating in a scarred society about to go up in flames, or so it seemed, Ratch took his cues from the Beats, from underground comic books, from the Kool-Aid acid lingo of the times. Much of the poetry then, written by Allen Ginsberg, Ed Sanders, and Lawrence Ferlinghetti, eschewed formalist writing and shocked the establishment with funky themes and four-letter words. Sanders actually went to prison for publishing his magazine *Fuck You: A Magazine of the Arts.*

These iconoclast poets were echoed by other artists who developed a tabloid art. Ron Crumb's outrageous *Zap Comix* led the way, as did Andy Warhol's films with their semiverbal characters speaking like figures in comicstrips—if it couldn't be gotten inside a balloon, forget it! And if what was said was mindless—so what? Pretend that a vision had transpired, a vision eluding establishment creeps. Warhol's characters spoke as if half their brains had sizzled away, burnt out by dope. The minimal became a means of protesting a sick culture; to be parsimoniously verbal was to bug the establishment. You were then much less communicative with the enemy, who were unable to reach your depths of conscience and feeling and make you vulnerable.

Ratch's poetry has connections with this protest culture; and it relates also to the Existentialists, who were much read and admired at the time. Albert Camus's heroes seem tragic because their minimalist speech entraps them. Samuel Beckett's abstract figures stumble around in a wasteland looking for Godot and the remotest hint that life has any meaning. Both nature and man are utterly wasted.

I simplify. But it does help to understand Ratch's work, if we recall the sixties as a decade when many revolutionary currents channeled themselves into a vigorous stream of protest screaming for basic reversals in our mores.

These several currents are reflected in Ratch's earliest poems. *Puppet X*, a doll without a name, operated by strings only partially defined, speaks of a wasted culture and seems to avoid suicide by emitting his thoughts in half-formed gasps. His speech resembles that inside balloons in comicstrips. He talks as if he's made of cardboard, not flesh. He employs a crazy, devastating humor that turns macabre and ironic. Life is a matter of sheer existence amid irrationality and pain. When T.S. Eliot wrote of our going round and round that mulberry bush as a mindless action in a world seen as a mindless wasteland, he was envisioning life in similar terms.

Clown Birth resembles *Puppet X* in its drift. There is a central narrative presented with utter economy — Ratch's clown has little breath to waste, and his observations, while they are spare in breath, do not spare his culture. Consider his notion that simply by being born we are born as clowns (clones?). We are superficial figures harboring enormous interior deserts of angst. On that surface, our painted-on smiles and happiness face-dots belie what is really transpiring in our hearts and souls. A clown's interior life, in its anguish, is probably very like a puppet's interior life.

After *Clown Birth* Ratch seemed to sense that changes were necessary. With *Osiris* we can see that that change was towards a poetry of pure language. The narrative elements present in *Puppet X* and *Clown Birth* have shriveled into mere abstract hints of place and event. Obviously, *Osiris* suggests ancient Egypt and ritual cults; and our placing the Osiris poems in this historical context is important. This is in itself fascinating, for it serves Ratch as a paradigm for writing poetry so spare that he seems to have chiseled it on slabs of stone.

Again, both his *grammar* and his philosophy merge. Passion is kept at a distance, except insofar as a play of language allows it to enter. In one of the *Osiris* poems, gouged-out eyes and tomb bats are surprises, suiting an ancient theme of lost kingly power and maimed pride, perhaps terrifying us—but only after the grammar of the poem has asserted itself.

Helen, published here for the first time, contains ancient motifs—Helen of Troy as paramour and destructive agent. Ratch continues to be parsimonious with his lines. We read them as if we were reading short breaths translated from ancient stele. The fragility of the poems evokes a timelessness, a runic quality. Here, Ratch's earlier comic-strip humor is gone, as are the Existentialist commentaries. Art, it appears, now assumes its own reason for being; and if poet and audience do indeed sit on the edge of a precipice, just before the final hydrogen blast, to celebrate Osiris and Helen in such hesitatingly lovely, brief lines generates an ironic distance.

Ratch's turns towards the old poet Geoffrey Chaucer and to the modern Ezra Pound are further thrusts towards a pared poetry. Ratch's art now becomes "Marginalia." If in his first books he was writing half-completed inscriptions on stone, he is now writing lists of words as "poems" in the margins of other men's poems. The poet now seems to be urging himself out of existence; his presence remains only as a hand holding a pen, a seemingly disembodied hand scribbling down gasps/words in the murky depths of the night. *Chaucer Marginalia* is an experiment toward this end. It is refreshing, however, to find that *yCantos*, inspired by Pound, is a blend of the marginalia mode and the stele mode of *Osiris* and *Helen*.

I include Jerry Ratch early in this series because he illustrates so well what a host of poets of his generation are doing: viz., the Language Poets in the San Francisco Bay Area and on the East Coast. Ratch, though, is of no coterie; his poems stand on their own as fascinating excursions into the contemporary spirit, and into pure poetry. I hope that numerous readers will find beauty in his work. Ratch requires that we linger, reading the poems aloud, allowing them to echo, in a kind of advanced listening chamber with acutely sensitive receiving systems.

I have asked Ratch to supply a note about his methods, a practice not generally followed in our series.

His remarks are helpful, and should assist readers puzzled by his experiment. Finally, while we have named the various parts of the book after his titles, in every case his books are represented by selections and do not appear in their entirety.

Robert Peters
Editor, *Poets Now*

AUTHOR'S NOTE

I first began writing *Marginalia* because I couldn't write at the time & didn't know what else to do. My effective vocabulary after having finished *Osiris* consisted of the two words, Hand and Glove. On a whim, and out of boredom with not writing for about one year, I had the good fortune to be reading "The Miller's Tale" in the *Norton Anthology*, which somehow I had never really read before. I was working in a paint factory at that time; it was winter, things were slow, I could read in short bursts between things I had to do, without getting caught. In short, brevity was a necessity. Soon my eye would linger out among the words beside the body of Chaucer's text more than I could get myself to stay inside the tale; and soon my eye began to drift down this stringy column of words in the margin; and soon I began to speed through these too. And it began to get interesting: ejecting a few words here & there, misreading now & then, quick takes, like riffs. Then I started writing these experiments down. Soon I was on my way. Within three months I had about six-hundred pieces to work with. Then I began to modulate the concept from that base.

Chaucer Marginalia was the result of this first group. I then started working with any marginalia I could get my hands on. The Anonymous Ballads, Spenser, whatever editors were kind enough to provide. The interesting thing, in particular, to me was that my possibilities of word usage had increased suddenly & so tremendously, partly because I felt released into a new world war of words and had been freed from the tight rule and old law of Singularity, and had learned how to walk out into the newfangledness of Multiplicity. I had also learned how to read *Vertically*.

Helen is the result of these marginalia sideswipes on material other than Chaucer, but combined with a bent and honed more toward a completeness, a feeling, a tonality. And finally, the pieces grouped under the term *yCantos* are glosses on some of the *Cantos* of Ezra Pound. y equals "function of" in mathematics.

Jerry Ratch
Berkeley, California

CONTENTS

Puppet X   1

Clown Birth   59

Osiris   87

Helen   105

Chaucer Marginalia   139

yCantos   165

PUPPET X

"Saw John Fox again yesterday, still walking.
Been walking that way since World War II . . ."

I

I know you,
ladies & gentlemen

We see the near future
thru you

Your factual face
as you sit indoors

Youthless
In your ordinary chair

　　　"Mice run thru their vision
　　　Mice run thru the plot
　　　O la la
　　　& memory
　　　is a lot . . ."

I, also,
have memories

One afternoon
I was myself

II

It's important to sound
human, I know

To get fragile
near your
mother

I myself
get glimpses
now & then

> Once:
> eating chicken, staring
> at the inside
> of a muscle

> Once
> during a bad thunderstorm
> while running down the stairs
> with a stick
> to beat off the
> survivors

& again
when I had such a fever

that I was off
in a dangerous century

I began to suspect
the reason the trains kept
growing in the basement

Without terror
or beliefs

    The telephone rang
    & then the dog
    sang . . .

I saw how we had been
all arranged

Now we're narrow
& unreal

I am not required
to speak

One day I discovered I couldn't wake up again
& I've gotten used to it

III

I look good
together

Got these penny wings
I could actually fly with

It all becomes so clear

Sound goes down
Sanity returns in an instant
The night is bigger . . .

I'd rather stay near the ground
I'm not a practising angel

I see more
than you . . .

A piece of hair to you
is a snake to me,
& snakes are mean worms
to a giant, like a tree

Think how much less
a giraffe can see
with her face among the leaves

Or an airplane, a very high,
serious airplane
A jet is out of the question

& a rocket
is like a flea . . .

I'd rather push a pebble around

IV

I'm not a practising angel,
ladies & gentlemen

Got these penny wings
out of boredom

I need to know
that black & grey place
inside an angel
where you bow your head,

when a puppet
forgets himself,

when a man learns
how small deer laugh

—that we live
    singing about lettuce—
    blue lettuce on Thursday . . .

    (when they turn over a card
    & hand you a rule)

    "a bunny may weep
    a bunny may sleep

    & a big bunny
    may pray
    once in awhile . . ."

For I must spend time with them

& we will have our hours
ready

V

    It's true

    When a man goes mad
    ropes come down from the clouds

    He cannot be sure of anything
    Anything

The way's uncharmed
He thinks someone else's strange thoughts

& it all seems a simple trick
Like someone standing all night
on the back doorstep

—The Sea of White Time

—The wet sky
(which, said the pheasant,
does exist)

> "Sleep will tell you
> a pretty green story"
> O heart
>   If you return . . .

Or you're stuck in the traffic
& giant butterflies
light on the fenders
& stagger inside
your windows
(& kiss the ones that live)
in that medieval
way

The hopelessly married
in their cars

The nondescript of
every description
The old & apologetic

—They're all dead, mind you

Their names departing
from them & their children alike

& the butterflies don't
find too much delight
in all the cold
familiar faces

The necessity of rules
& jewels
& matters of the chest . . .

They would have lived simply,
given birth,
& fallen back into the earth—

If it had not been for the horror
of the passage . . .

& at the same time
the carrots are
kicking them in the ass

saying
Have a good
time,
kids

VI

Welcome to the
pain & amusement park

The lowered hurdles,
the galleries of sleep

I know it hurts you all
to see me here

Believe me, it hurts me too

You didn't exactly expect bullets
did you
We aren't all human
Ask about

  — Dogs talking
      of stupidity
  — Geese honking before time

11

— Cows

Cows don't know a Sunday from
a Monday, what do cows know

Clearly these are not human

Take the one in front of you
He wants to bleed
without getting himself wet

Does this seem
strange & familiar
somehow

Looking into all the possible
night windows

You think they are alive
& you try getting them
to speak

But you see it's no use

— Emotionally asleep

.   .

Sons of the sleepless
Postured gentlemen (gentle swans)
Daughters of the dead
How we dream!
We do

    .   .

You bow & come before
the farmer or the judge
& repeat what
was expected of you
Rule, reason, prayer

    "I might have made it
    thru the day, if
    she hadn't let down
    her hair

    It would've been all right
    I know it . . ."

Your reasons

You keep boiling them down
Boiling them down
Boiling them down

Till the vat goes
poof

Or you work for the publishers
until your brain becomes
a lima bean

& then you smoke your pipe
& think about
that . . .

Have you ever had the true
laughter
driven out of
your body

Have you ever seen
a small white cloud form
within easy reach

(Have you ever seen the dwarfs
perform)

Have you

       —bugs with their
         puny faces

    —giant butterflies trying to sleep
      on a train

    —clown birth

      ?

It used to be a laugh
Now it's a signal

The specimens are speaking,
ladies & gentlemen

We all have party hats on . . .

Let us reach
underground &
remember

    —The lick that
      starts the ice

    —The wax that will

The hands that
put us thru our motions . . .

Then we'll sit down
in old chairs

I want you to
face the toys
Ladies & gentlemen

Before someone
has killed someone real

See the scars
the burns
the terror

VII

I had a friend once
Little weak flame
of a voice
No bigger than
an ordinary tulip
Pure cowboy

You see him in all the old photographs
(In his 1 dollar shirt
& his 2 dollar hat)

The most popular song
offended him so much
that he would tap his foot to it
He would tap his foot
& begin spitting out bitter,
imaginary pieces
of tobacco

— His reflections
    are still in
    the windows

He fell in love
with the Queen of Clubs
& he can't get back alive . . .

Now he talks nonsense & gets away
with it

        He's got friends
        in the 4th dimension

I saw there
a sign that said:

No Smoking
no opium

What would start out a usual bird
would turn out to be
an eagle or a hawk

None of them sang anymore
They'd just eat . . .

& a storekeeper said
They're all dead here

& when I looked
there weren't any cans on the shelves
Just skulls

We were turning around to leave
& he said:
        You'll be dead too . . .

& in the neighboring town of
Virden, Ill, passing thru
one night, I saw a man
sitting in a gas station
intently watching the candy machine . . .

Tell me
What did his soul
look like
My friend's

— A pinched nerve in twilight

— A few scattered
   bones on the moon

If that . . .

The glass is melting slowly
from his feet

      "& once an ant, half red,
      the back half
      black,
      tried speaking to me

      & kept looking behind it"

Hell

Kittens can spot
an obvious ghost

I can see again, said the farmer
I can see again, said the judge

(& that's as big as nebulous
gets)

I'd rather be your uncle
I'd rather sleep
alone

This is ridiculous
said the goldfish
What an outrage
thought the clam

Well we all know
it is . . .

This believing in things

caskets, cradles
delivery tables
scalpels, shears
& throats

caskets, cradles
delivery tables,
scalpels,

shears,
& throats

Before you know it you die
Before anyone notices
you pick yourself up & keep going
Pretty soon you've even fooled yourself

In this kind of evil,
small-watt light
sums of money are exchanged,
signs are given, nods, etc.
Contracts made to snuff out
candles . . .

    "We're all here,
    aren't we"

A small crowd
under the wallpaper
saying things

(while you sleep)
(while you sleep)
Blue the Bunny
while you 2 sleep
X Y Z

X Y Z
X Y Z
(pass it on)

Things written down
For you

— The world is kind
— The world is cruel

& Johnny's a drummer
& drums for the king

"It's not necessarily your story"
"It's not necessarily their story"
& everywhere you go
that's what the clocks say:
Nobody in particular

& now the dead
spider hangs
on the underside of
the book

    "Because I could change
    the scenery"

& now
the dead spider
drifts slightly overhead
in what's left of
the blue
& the lightning

"Because I could change . . ."

& now the dead spider
is running the
world

la de da   la de da
Let Spider come over

Dead Spider is
running the world

"Oh, oh"

Dead Spider
is running
the world

VIII

After too much
I had forgotten how to fly.
There was a small owl with me
on the old dirt road by the wind.
It was a very dark grey,
like an ash.
Its beak moved, it opened & shut,
opened & closed,
but I had also forgotten the language
of owls.
I could see that its wings
were too short
& it too could not fly,
but it had never
forgotten how.
And it saw
that I no longer understood.
Two times I tried simply
leaning into the wind,
& both times I flopped on the ground.
& the small owl waddled over to me
& it peered into my face
& its beak moved
& moved,
but it did not speak.

IX

It seems useless to dream
Daydream

    :big influential chairs
    :clouds carrying the water
    without disturbance

(the invisible toys of sleep . . .)

How many a man
can have

—a man saying: I am king

Still, something had stood up
inside me . . .

I was
myself

Honest

X

Still
I don't know

One minute you're
squeezing the brains out of
goldfish, the next
you're running the
show

After awhile
it's hard to raise an eyebrow over
anything

   — the sound of
     lightly falling souls
   — your crotch cold & dreaming:

     pneumonia   oldmonia
     6 is half a dozen

Is the way you
would say it
I suppose . . .

It shouldn't
have to be
that way

—raised to forget quickly
—smiling around

—used to being artificial

The dead dislike themselves
The living
are in pain

What hopelessness, misery,
despair
One thinks of washing his hands
One doesn't care . . .

We know   the rules   we know

—the road to Standard City

XI

They've got prizes for you,
my dears. Yes they do

You'll see yourself accepting

I know how happy
you'll be

O yes   O no
You ain't so bad

O yes

Necktie white shirt the usual

    —But always
       right at the edge
       of his smile,
       there was pain . . .

There's no need to talk
of death

       the overheated seaweed
       gulls on fire

Whole roomfuls
dying like they don't know it

Your mind
shrivelled with sleep

—Once said to live

My wig, your wig

I smiled
I didn't hear a word
he said, you
understand
But I smiled . . .

I smile
I bend
at the waist
I'd hate to be human
here

    Aren't we having fun

    Yes we are . . .

XII

One day I discovered
I couldn't wake up again

O yes

I used to sleep

(& wear beautiful dresses
among them)

Day or night
Didn't matter

Dumb & happy

An umpire

Giving
impressions of owls

Big party
Good time

Life ain't so easy to find
anymore

We all have party hats on

I insist

XIII

What have they done with us

30

Even the witnesses
were choked
Where I have been

People laugh & people die
& they avoid a man who
says
he is lonely

Convinced of the possession
of themselves

They'll kiss the statues
goodnight
& then continue
in a conversation
with someone I
honestly can't see

There's no explaining it . . .

We live
We look into mirrors
Ladies are drowning in heaven

Another kick in the ass
by a passing cloud

—The collar comes up
  around their ears

—You're still
  alone

I saw one
drunken
old old man
without a chin
sweeping out a barn

& every time he'd
knock a cobweb down
he'd say:
Take that, Florence

The town you were born in
& lived for awhile

& all died young
Trying to keep in line

The way it's going
we'll all have to become —

O God, O dresses

They must *tell* us
we're good

No more sensibility
than a clam —
& even that's going too far . . .

Actually
worms are needless here

Nobody cares
whether you sing
or sleep

No matter what

    No matter

Not exactly dead
yet

& yet, not asleep
not asleep

Certainly not
asleep

But the new years do
glide by unnoticed

All the same

The world takes no walk

XIV

We thought we saw
Once

We thought if we could
just make it thru
the business of growing up

We thought things like glass
were normal

& trees fell for no reason

—Otherwise the skin would fly off
in one great sheet

—Otherwise the skin would
fly off the planet

Is what that is . . .

I saw a bug standing up
in a drop of water

I saw myself
far away
in a window

The swan
on earth

You're not supposed
to look

How could I ever

XV

Suppose
I look

& suppose I
do

Standing on my own

Glass headache
in my hand

The crushed moth
That could have taken you
to the moon

The ant
sees

I believe this . . .

I won't get any smaller

XVI

When we lie down
under the wind

the trees swaying
looking out over the fields

soft cobweb of a brain

exposed to hail
exposed to snow

trying to back away
from it

unable

knowing the earth
(the face it will take)

our names
fluttering loose
& sleep spreading over the planet —

the wind that
makes a candle
flicker & the
flame go to hell —

the full moon will rise
on this gust
& swerve over the
horizon

trees will know
the names of women

the ones we knew

there will be hilarity
among machine guns

daggers become ribbon

bullets
the worm we love

bridge river trees

when we are in our grave

The saucer will rattle
& the teacup dance

XVII

Clouds float past
the local moon

Somebody opens
an old wooden door

The lights go out
They come back on

& you say it's
only the wind?

The North rolls up
on the horizon

    We shall see
    We shall see

I could let that bother me

The moon is back
again
We can't be sure . . .

    Who we are

Don ?
Don't remember

XVIII

The goldfish is dead
& the clam went away

I saw that the goldfish was dying
A bulge in his side
& his double tailfins hanging down

So I put his bottle in the sunlight
on the windowsill
where I could watch
the sun on his golden body
& the light blue
at the ends of his double fins
It was like catching
a tiny pair of angel's wings

I watched his body turn sideways
That bloated side about to burst

I watched as his body rose
thru the vegetation
Past the red & brown snail
dreaming of wood

& I watched him
float to the surface &
kiss the day goodbye

XIX

Those that I carried

The exposed

Their little burned suitcases

Bodies emerging
from the wind

You all know

I mean
that you see them

Their skins
coming to the surface

The spinal night . . .

Can they be called fires

They went into
their flaming colors
& closed the doors

White silence
The vessels of emotion
      Then too hot, then too cold

Nobody comes
from there

XX

Who can sing
anymore

Steam coming from every light switch
& fixture in the nation

The loud apathy
in the pines

Diddle diddle diddle
All you can do

Or give a good dog your hand . . .

Juries of yes
& no . . .

1 or 2 light taps
on the shoulder

All it takes

What could they possibly
have to say
In the light of science & restraint

A man conducting business
in a straight jacket
Begging your pardon
& eating his sleeves

—He let out with
    this massive bow-wow

        —He's trying to live . . .

How odd

        We will have to
        watch each other
        very closely

Ah, yes
The ability to

Hands with labels
on them

Your clothes & passes

        Bracelet Bracelet
        on my wrist
        Give my face
        another twist

Oh, oh
You blew your wishes out

So long, flames

You aren't going to get
flesh from the radio . . .

Fragments to the universe . . .

The audience is quiet
The bridge is singing

XXI

I see
I see things
differently

The ugly side
The pretty side
The people in
their beds

Guessing at angels
from under a tree

I was certain

I was certain, determined
& mean

Now I'm not
so sure

These woods
These weeds
This particular slope . . .

My language is alive, & my eyes
Though my heart is sometimes cold
I admit

Though we try all
our disguises
& act
perfect

We are not actors
We are parodies
A corpse going
over hurdles

We don't get far . . .

Now I am nothing
I have given in

I knew it wasn't me

I laughed
I laughed so hard
I broke my foot

Causing a long sensation
of feeling

& lay there like a piece
of something that had gone wrong

O I don't act normal

I laughed all the way thru it
I forgot & grew old

The dog barking all the time
like an annoying heartbeat

A noise to live with . . .

I notice the room
It seems very close

There they are
calling each other
by their names

> Oh, he's alive & laughing
> somewhere on earth
> Rest assured . . .

Having to stand around in garages

Diminished

Useless

While people rake their lawns
in the world

Tiny balloons to ants

Happiness to the clothesline

Light laughs
over the surface of things . . .

Don't think me dust
Just yet

Pale & lawless

I like it on earth

It rained hard
All the roses
were face
down

I saw a thing
pulling a black hankie
out of its side

Adhesive

All those things

      Conclusions to be had

      Life is here . . .

Little messages coming in

Stars breaking thru
the myths of body

Into the sea of
unwilling skin

My unbegotten children
My daughters, my sons

XXII

& so
Goodbye to flowers
Goodbye to the purple iris
Considerations
Of time & pansies
    afternoon
    glass (4pm)
    hillside

Of life
of what the desolate imagination
makes of it

Of what is
to come
for someone in this room

Because
you'll forget who you are
Who you were
or wanted to be

    This is going to
    make me dance

Your obnoxious soul

Pestering twilight
with its presence . . .

Somebody put a head on the body
& an arm, & a leg
& stuck it all back together again

Then it sat up & said, Hello . . .

Ah, the sweet cardboard
As it's never been

XXIII

A powdery wind
issued out of factories

The spirit in pain
in the near wood

—It shouldn't make sense

We're all inhuman, sometimes

Some more than others

& some can't get back
again . . .

Pretty soon
nobody will remember

Chill, sweat, chill
I grew so weak
I met death three times
On the carpet
& in the hall
& once again
I stared into the toilet
thinking of hatchets
& the will to live
I walked around
in a large nameless circle

    . . . giving my address: . .

& got so cold
I stuffed my useless
rubbery arms
into my pockets
like the souls of ducks

Big yellow plastic mice
that walk upon me
& then give me a
15 min lecture on

how friendly the mice of California
were

Little ventures
into space

Fate
In a cheerless cobweb

>Parlors in the moon
>Parlors in the moon

>Parlors in the moon
>shine

Bright & daily
contact
with those on earth
It's what I need, O

Radio

XXIV

No wind, big storm
Lightning in the desert
In the mind

You have no name
& now you're
no one

—Is this the new law

The dead are pulling up their dresses

& I,
I've brought my passport, my dears

It says
I am the kelp of the angels

& it gets me around . . .

I'm terrified
to get this way

Who can tell
what I am

The rose alone

O yes

XXV

The puppet came to me
& he smiled

(We will not whisper
 about it . . .)

I see it now

My life, your life
(the water running down)

    Is it death
    Is it dreamless

Its sleep
was like a white cotton thread

All evening, & into the night,
I felt dead
I felt like I *had* to move around
to keep up appearances

You don't want to laugh

"Like a true balloon
 he wobbles his head"

Now we don't have to worry
about running out
Now we don't have to worry
about running in
Upstairs
Downstairs
Now we're drinking gin

Well
I know him
Yes

The owl & the umpire
Run where you will

— Hopeful little smiles
   drawn on their faces

— The owl asking
   the same bare thing
   of every
   one

XXVI

When I dream again
(the invisible things of sleep

attaching themselves to me)
O heart
     So immortal —

I can't tell you

Let the flesh ashore
To see what went right

There's got
to be more

Let them lie there
Let them soften

Not trying to move
or hold anything

Let them often hear
your voice, the wind
back before the waves
ever occurred

Vague space memories

The corners of time
in a light rain

This is all
I know

Once I
was like you

I went into my room
& crawled under the bed

I repeated my sins . . .

    You don't have much time
    before you'll
    be fooled

—The natural clam
  shall desert the heart

& pure death a thing
from the past
An eerie laughter
across the prairie . . .

Sometimes
I hear equations, O
Gentle Swans, O Gentleswans
My country sleeps with thee

CLOWN BIRTH

We have come only to sleep
We have come only to dream
It is not true, it is not true
We have come to live on the earth

—from a Nahuatl poet

I

*

fully
torn by this hour
driving home
under darkness

how the mind hardens
into a kind of knot
while the day drags on

dreams of no avail

the first particles of
sleep drifting in
bad moments of unending clarity

*

fog cuts the top
off grizzly peak
makes it look like
an important mountain

fire under the earth
eager the dragon

13 seconds to have a drink
turn around
& fly away

then they blow wind
up & down your spine

*

friend
in the petrified forest

sown shut

there's what they call Fall
here

it's not autumn

black stars upon the road

two bugs

in a glass corner

where bees & flies
die daily

*

there's no need
to hide anything
there are still men sad enough
to drink with their heads down

night music
I never heard

lovers

others . . .

I sat & talked
with the visionary
carrot

big posters

softly
the birds
lay their heads
on the ground
& softly beat their
wings

my sword it lies broken
& lies in a lane

*

I can balance anywhere

I could achieve poise
on the head of a pin

elevation

el. 593
pop: 0

raised desert

11 am

road

*

you're going to
wear a hole thru
your reasoning
at this rate

rainy mouse
in the year 3000
after the logical wars

monitors listening in
to the end

why I remember I don't know

funny

*

when I was young
I shot a bird

it looked at me
it looked at me
but did not say a word

sentimental purple
twilight
rose of my hand

holding God
rocking

*

I thought: the machine shall not determine
you don't belong in people's backyards
you don't steal people's turtles

waiting for that cosmic
pat on the back

like a dog
strumming his heart

*

he wants to drink
where people drink

I shift my position
let's face it
this means terror in the beginning
terror in the end
& terror thruout

*

Ballade

when I was young
I shot a bird
my shrunken heart doth flower
the bird flew down
& hit the ground
& looked at me one hour

it looked at me
it looked at me
but did not say a word

& as it fell
I went to hell
& shot another bird

II

*

they have stepped into
a shade no one else
can see

& this a broken
window
upon the big night

ignorance of the eyes
no excuse
they ran into

didn't realize how
1 2 3 4 5 6
7

busy it was

green smoke
from a witch's
coat

goodnight everyone
else why
goodnight.   I love

*

rat in the sun
rat in the sun

*

standing up in utah
strong whisper
ah, the worm
made me do it
yes
my mad face
cross & mean
& tight
the need to
cry, night
night

*

there's an expression
bears are thinking about
leaves falling from

68

two states away
laughter, hollow, colored little
smokes
hot feathery points of the stars

under the bed
this year
senility comes early

without any teeth (or mind)
or claws

but it can still sit
on you

*

voices
this morning
many of them

moss & vine
the markings on
the walls

still
love in you
only that noise

a large wing
out of me
in a tree

of all places

wing in the orchard
wind
the separate chamber

a sense of real
waddle waddle nothingness

I've forgotten
sparrow

I have been a thin animal

that won't do

*

in six months
I'll get fat
leave the feathers
in my mouth

70

the thing ran
into the night
with its own soul
the blue jay said it
I didn't
who started
a fire in the trees

*

the peculiar behavior
of certain shrubs
each leaf
part of a long
letter
somehow I have lost

connections I know
I must have had
the hurriedly sketched
history of the earth

*

we have a hard time hearing
wells anymore

live on horses
by memory

kick bugs in the head
our witness

of course
that's what sobriety does
for the soul

I shouldn't tell

*

the flea inside your sock
the piece of plastic
in the grass
fallen nearby
which heard us smiling

nothing noticed
ocean flattened
the candles won't blow out
the cats are
ah, listen to them
with their natural
howls they are

*

a bird came along
& started a fire

on an alligator
who was laughing out loud
I turn the rump of disgust
on the entire matter
bees were looking
at the ladies
spider webs were
raised to greet us
oysters begetting oysters   Oooo!
it took a big
kick to bring us
around

*

people getting killed, dirty water,
chances of war
seaweed on the
walls of the ocean
the evening animal
of misery
look who smells
O look who smells
may a wind come up

I suppose getting
out of bed
is the answer

*

now the lobster
turns his tiny face
toward you
for perhaps the
first time
during the entire
conversation

*

if I were a serious fish
in the ocean
too scared to get out
on earth no
tree
before laughter   before
warm treasure
& reason
red bows
broken china
shotgun gut & weed . . .

amusement
under my heart
where that thought
began

amusement
a subtle comment
by a little duck
& yes
truthtelling

*

to the lady whose laughter
was rolling heavily
in a storm

I suppose getting out of bed
is the answer, said the oyster

I suppose, said the pearl

I suppose

if that rotten laughter
is what's driving us

*

Angel, 1508

when bees die they die
with their wings straight out
they die of natural causes

& their tiny bodies are bent
as though landing on
a flower

their wings seem
too big for them
& they lie scattered
about the floor, tilted
in dead positions

now you have no
life, are tilted
forward that way
no noise from you
no danger in your stinger
no testimony

the way your body's bent
hunched up
singed with ecstasy

*

Durer

columbine, 1525, looks the same
the weed thrown in, the same
unchanged . . . 1525 & nothing's

changed. wars have not yet
occurred among plants. they don't
throw rocks, that is. sling guns

& good good health to you. you look
the same. you have not changed. you
have not changed at all.

III

If you don't believe, just look at September,
    look at October!
The yellow leaves falling, falling, to fill both
    mountain and river.

—Zenrin poem

*

an american indian (in a suit) at
the museum reception, eating pelican wing
which looked like enlarged sections of
older pulpy (pink) grapefruit

when asked why he was eating this,
he said that eating pelican wing gave you

the ability to fall from a great height
without injury

   instead the body simply absorbed
the earth's knowledge at that particular
spot

*

the souls of dead executives
lunch freely on rotting meat
& organic deposits on the lawn

how does a pair of wings
get connected to such things

that fly's an asshole

the asshole of a dead man
I believe

*

for a minute I thought
that was my house
reconstructed
for a minute I thought you
put it up again

took a picture
& then knocked it over
for a minute
the trees existed
for a minute
there was grass
the grapevine
my brother in the bushes
with the girl next door
the moonlight on the lawn
the lightning coming from the west
the men & women running
shooting
the one peaceful sweep
of neutrons

*

the stars stayed red
where angels
warm their hands
the sky blue
where one fell thru
no feather, no soul
lights out
nome alaska
song keep the wind
wind the fine ice

a tree out there
in heaven

*

an angel fell on its back
& everything around it
began to burn
comets in alleyways
the leaves yellow
& red
death speaks in low tones
& raises its hat
do you know where
jupiter is
not right this moment no

*

chicken over the ocean
look the other way
I opened my other eye
I saw the seasons passing
overhead
the future
I imagine everyone
noticed
take me into your
arms, god

I'm a duck
I used to be a seaweed
what went wrong

*

the only contact I seem to
have with earth
one tiny spot of backache
small comfort

IV

*

your houses
blessed with bees
this big, that big
alcohol revery
what is it
blue wave
what is it
pieces of crumpled stone
sitting on the steps
the brain a walnut
rattled

*

who's going to
clip the toenails
of God
who will plume the chicken
who tend
the little flower
of the soft person
who steal the pea out
from under the bank
while you're holding it up
O the felt hats
of heroism
who'll say that
arizona snowflake
who'll say that
atomic beef jerky
the mobility of
Jane
who that
who that

*

someone you knew
part of whose face appears
in a mouse's ear
flies that keep
landing on you

nasty & cruel hour
where you tie &
untie your bathrobe
five & six times
a minute
serene insect
gripping your heart
you look at it
because you are insane
closing your eyes
doesn't make it
dark

*

no smoking in the
meadow
no smoking in
the mirror
forest without trees
no smoking there
public urinals
no smoking there
the last thing I saw
was 180 dark shadows
taken to the stars

*

83

I see whenever we say
wheeze & bubble & ooze
we mean corpse
not chorus
remember that death
is brightness no
illumination no
I only have
as much time as
I will need
no
recollection

*

drunk on my lunch hour
brain used up
niggling after pennies
middle of the week
the day of the
mitten
raise your hand
boyscout
I will not lie
I will not steal
which can lead to
death & dizzyness
yes
& chocolate flame vaginas

*

I saw a big dog
by the side of the road
I saw a small deer by
the side of the road
the failure of rock
a little maroon water
driving home
under darkness

the wind is
under a rose
right now
new blood will
fill the earth
we must love the months
available

till we see again

make the sun rise
the air forget
& do it
with a minimum
of singing

OSIRIS

the patient man
is sitting on the drift
watching his sins pass by
& sees the river reed
mocking
the reed of the plain
saying:
when the grass is burning
the other one laughing also
saying:
when the river fills up

(*Basuto, African*)

*

the soul was pictured as a bird
with a human's head and blue &
black wings
    I have seen the soul resting
in a tree, looking down at me
    & even if I am a reed in a ditch
or even the tree the soul sits in
    or the jackal laughing in the desert
or the jackal laughing in the street
    or mad, even mad & broken by slavery:
I shall come back, with my bird's head,
my costume, & my human's eye

*

so it was
the soul that was
called back

in that sudden
beating of wings

said Run
but my heart
was not there

said Run
but my heart was
in the way

*

heart ruined & dry
running with a dry sound
left on the bank
& dry clack of reeds

short glance back
then west
toward the meager hills
following the shadow

head down
hanging in the sky

over the plain
& up the warming
slope of the hills

*

but
imagine the violence
within

& within the wind
now enemy service,
riding freely

whose touch stretches
from reed to reed

baking with madness,
and burning

*

when he died
I heard his name
running down the halls

people carried it
in their mouths
like wool, like cotton
& cats came
when they heard it

the red moon rose
while a warm
uncommon wind blew
off the desert
& scorched the land
& our grain with it

seven years we were blasted
and we heard the wild dog laugh
& come in closer

& at night
we could hear them
outside the door
laughing, carrying off the
children of the dying
& the children of the dead

& the red moon rose
over & over
making the night transparent
making it thin

*

what does he feed on
only what he sees
what does he feed on
only what he sees

what does he live on
what he eats
what does he live on
what he eats

who are his attendants
tomb bats
that fly in the night

o who has
gouged out his eye

and who has made him
not to speak

that he might diminish
decrease
& gradually lose power

*

entered the chamber & as we descended
the ladder into the pit, where the king
lay surrounded by the things that were
with him during his reign,
  remarked the figures on the walls
around us, how one was looking out
at the viewer, with her hand held up
as though waving,
  so close, though really it was just
a hand that was waving from behind a
chorus of women in profile, singing,
or wailing

*

Kept walking along
the edge of the highway
I was
looking for a way
to earn a living
The soldiers were
rushing past me,
& the priests
They were looking for
tomb robbers
& I was one

I was one
I was one

*

on the road we came upon one who proclaimed
himself king, and portions of two royal necklaces
dropped by a thief, and procured from him his
confession signed with his own hand and herein
enclosed

and this same then led us to the place where
his fellows were busy with other articles of
obvious royal treasure, which they immediately
admitted as belonging to this self-proclaimed
king already in our care and custody, so
surprised were they at our sudden appearance
(our swiftness)

and as I have already reported, the wine seals
in the tomb broken, the wine drunk to emptiness,
and this we believe led the thieves to their
demise, being boastful and sloppy

and have procured further testimonials, proofs
and confessions (also enclosed), whereupon they
were dealt with and sent West without ceremony
and left for the jackals and the hawks

there is the matter of one other of whom they
spoke briefly, too shadowed a figure and too
fugitive to make out exactly as to description
or whereabouts, which no amount of torture
or promise of leniency could secure, and which
may account for the items at large, and for

which reason I suggest we repack and reseal
the offended King's tomb and return to leisure
and sure sport

*

& then the queen sent a message
saying
I am told you have grown-up sons
send me one of them
and I will make him my husband
and he shall be king
to which he replied
where is the son of the late king
and what has become of him
and she replying hastily
(there being but little time left)
why should I deceive you
I have no son, and my husband is dead
send me a son of yours and
I will make him king
But it was too late

*

the room illumined by
that light

& the lamp
(especially the neck of it)

.   .

& while they sat
& while we danced
for them

they in that eternal room
illumined by late
sunlight

our skin
moistened with oils
glistening

each of us shining
as we turned
emitting little

rivers of light

& while we worked
while we sweated

& our perfumed odors
rose
in the heavy air

under stone
limestone & granite

while the kingdoms
changed hands
& we danced

while the kingdoms
changed hands
& we danced

*

   and the wall they had built between them
and the queen raised her daughter in her own
house while he had his different women in,
but upon occasion they would be seen in their
boat on the lake
   and then the king died
   and the queen had suitors then, for the queen
may not rule alone, & she had outlived him

   and who was this god for whom you built a
city

*

the offering no longer
visible

how someone had
gouged out the face

how the offering
could no longer
be received

that the soul was
lost

& without purpose

that his reign
had ended

*

you did not seem so concerned with the
eternal when you were younger and your
father the king would have never let his
empire get brittle and would never ignore
his nobles in such a manner as this the
way you have, and took great pride in his
horsemen and in you yourself
    and now the empire has withered and has
dwindled and shrinks further than you know

*

their future beards
appearing in a dream

unspoken weariness
upon entering eternity

o little rain of pure
salt

the world beyond the hawk
will look so small

o little rain

white
& pure

*

it meant
a child would have to
run the world

& who can ask the king
to choose between war
and mechanical toys

when the king is only twelve

meanwhile our boat
floats upon the lake

& our religion, also

and our fate

*

o sunlight casting shadows
o last sunlight
on the hilltops
o late rose earth up there
o final underwater light
bathing the hills in thickness
o late sun setting
o light illuminating the halls
light falling on the western face
of houses along the streets
o bright walls aflame,
set breathing by the light
o western shore
burning

*

when I think I am
in the hands of the right
god

just as I am
entering the new queen

comes the voice
of the last one
calling me from behind
with the endless
blood of memory

Pharaoh, Pharaoh

*

we rowed across
the water to the west
sight passed
from sunken eye
to sunken eye
the golden day
drained from my wings
burned out
heading into beige
hills, west

*

102

whose soul
do you have

how many are
you

there are several
running from death,
laughing,

whom you might know

HELEN

HELEN

1

the young
that the sea took

kissing their lips

catching them
up
in its arms

hiding them
from each other

truly

listen to
its elevated, fleeting
thoughts near death

when
she carries out
her men

Of travel

of the Fates
high governors hidden
from us

crescent moon
that lies with
anyone

rain
As cheaply

*

interior
ill-pleased

the heart
at its center ill-pleased

taken
by the temple
of human possession

west wind
darkens the evening
girls   Youth   shore
Noise, courage, boldness

*

burned ahead
endured the flames

found
haughtiness had
little bearing
on the unbraided
thread
of pleasure

sweet venus
there hung

For just as we discussed
her

for you know
how her thread hangs

just as I owe it
to her

I felt it float
once
& bless me

just as she wished it

And praising
separated them

feasting
beneath her clothes

Because the sun
is aware of
flesh

*

heart returns
to another

I know how it burns

good cheer
& dreams kept me
awake

and other
little businesses
I've imagined

if it never
went out
it would soon
begin to lie

Joy
makes lovely mates
flow continually

I know
loudly
dampened hills
snakes/stones
creatures exiled
from wood
where the wind
leaps/breaks

*

them stories about her

big puffy ones
billowing upward

names with wisps of
white lie attached

providence

the end of life
leaving her body

how the well breaks

& a gust of wind
goes straight up
through her

*

behold
the more gentle ransom

how we do not know
the way she's wont to dress
that incites the noble
sun's uprising

how
she's pleased
with mixed intricate
emotions

*

delight
unlocks the gate

continually
changes the head
with the brittle poison
of curiosity

112

I led her
saw her again
secretly

on the morning
of the Sun

I thought
allow me the hour

limbs wet

though I am not
always ready

*

and of her custom,
and delight

does Oedipus
leave the nest

for him
tenderly
are the stones
confused

before him
grow cold

grief already dead

Yes

thought, time
do service
unto him

bound by
some accident
or chance

o wantonness
were you not
nobility
turned away

broken in two

by arrows assaulted

o guitar
ruined by
constant delight

*

reached down
into her clothes
to that excellent flow
where an ebony wind
fretted

great
blown up
many-headed magic
underneath its covering

food cheated muscles
recalling their sex

Look at
stupefying
womanhood passions

nor unbecoming

serious
after unchaste rejoicing

something final

spread out
perfumed

to pay back forever
the dark fear of
horrible nights
in childbirth

II

her wet golden look

Unbraided by
grief

Rubbed furrows
of original fleece

rolled in them
carved waves
on all sides

known malice
duplicity, doubleness

Because
if thou lie with
torture in the morning

that kind of
needless I am dying
sweat

immediately
the fever covers you

run mad
there'll be no help

*

in wet endeavor
they stood

passing the time

assuredly in pain

in this kind of
evening light

I will make the groves
Gaze on her

*

how the devil
ridicules
the blind berry of truth

how could he be so glad

117

unless
there were other wealth

goods
& safety
fly   by   in haste
& jeopardy

birds shining
in the evening

the lamp burning

no question
no plan

*

on earth
play
one time lovingly

then bathe

found
we could not
ward off
beat or uncover
its displayed lives

hyacinth
sapphire
ruby
squeezed with
hindrance

bristling forth

*

youths
who are accustomed
to those shores

who have heard
& believe in
the pagan sayings

who forsook
their religion
& felt death
ease against many

who take
kill   destroy
& live with strangers
in sin

but atone for
nothing
immediately
aboard ship
they rise

afraid to lose sight
of the shore birds

news of the shore

where
their unmerciful comrades

sound
the loud sound
with appealing
abandon

Draw them forth
on the agile beach

harping

begging
to be let go

from the grasp
of their song

o
graceful spirit, o
chaste flower of
temperance

Though by nature
she needs the devil
that birds handsome
& generous fly past

*

people say
care turns away
from the poor
at mealtime

in her
occasional
mid-day dress

listening to space

with a certain
darling control

They learn
her likeness

& the sweet
hesitation
that covers her neck

*

chant, sing of
the neck
how touch befalls its
pregnant knots
its ropes
teeming & filled

machine, engine, device
spread open
loosen
the shuddering country

her image
like a tow-headed statue

placed under her back
body & rear

Rise
sail

122

lord over
&
take me away

*

clearly
the planets gaze upon
such an end

Come the dice
with freedom

heard the malice
thrust about me

Noticing width
honor
the least

all the time
at the altar
wasted
monks hastened
sprinkling holy water

beseeching
yea   away   desires

Lie down with
profit & loss,
motive

balance the bubble
of sleep
on my tongue

in the desert
that
opens up
Young
Hotspur
goes riding

III

he had that quietness
by nature
fitting to
the art of healing

like a deer

parted
the fine quarters
of the world

inquiring into
this & that trouble

pain: none

driven away

though you prate
& rail

chatting with madness

*

asked him
about his demeanour

walked
dreamed great
awakened satisfaction

craft, favor, assurance

went through
the ruined day
that way

Awoke

the noble
opportunity of leisure

sighs
where troubled rocks
don't know the source
they must bear

although
he hid himself
in known beauty &
deserts
wept freely
over his duplicity

*

sat beside her
while she bathed

improper
talk of pleasure

knowing
what she seemed

lower

that certain mood

of destruction
implanted

that desolate place
in a satisfied
state of being

allowing
my eyes to feast on
her beauty

silver bracelets
around brown arms

not many
a few at the wrist

*

know
hot, feverish
she
children lounge
in every prosperous house

imagine worse

known sleepless
even if
from walking

prepared
glorious
ignorant
creature born of promise

when the thin
starve, something
anything
walks
livid, greenish
away

*

self
lullaby
pain

dark runs the lie

clothing above desire

in fresh pursuit,
in extravagant
daylight

with some
diaphanous material
over some parts of you

with things you like
made of silk

*

behavior
I might know
pulse heavy

spread out

rubies broke

beautiful looks
expression

chemise
decorated with pleats

thigh garment
loosened
hanging down

dignity
shot
breath
disordered

*

since every one
looks through
their own lament

thy neck Helen
bereft of fire

with due deliberation
sober men shall
call unnatural

glitter
might succeed
in rousing a few

but not you

you are not empty
of self control
and do not exult over
the held out heart

*

bustle & hurry
the gray, hoary crowd

impetuous, onrushing
many

wily & shrewd
causing many groans
rich in groans

crossing the sea
ah me

bestow upon us
— it is fated —
the dark grape
of divinity

drinking
ever
at any time
Anywhere

o foot
o heart mind soul

briars
retreat beside
men of prayer

if I judge correctly

while the sparrow
calls to the murderer
I who
I who

*

the storm
already together,
onslaught
its nature

that exults
in dim natural piercing

unbreakable
brass
continually moving
its surplus beauty

under the sun
marvelled at
by wise men

garments
of womanhood
on which wantonness
is based

vermilion
in appearance

drinking gardens
lovingly
spread out

*

took thought there

fashioned by
bright royal reds

eyes followed

went from
that dwelling
that region
of grey hundred men
tangled together
in unhappy pain

climbed
among the hills
where pale frozen sleet
fell

dragons

boars also

giants pursued

rode over the land

alone & without complaint

IV

    those who travelled
    with you
    arrogant   riding

    just for the cold thought
    of pleasure

    priests
    with elaborate eyes
    awakening
    with Satan in them

    newly bloomed

    eastern

&
unknown

*

exhausted

secluded shade
took off headband

raging
wild game

all fear passed

unconscious
deathlike

youth torch rage
over the defeated
earth

facial unlikeness
appearing to think

Of the sea
fruitless, vain

strange, foreign
from elsewhere

otherwise immortal
strong in both arms
shameless, pitiless
boundless, unfeeling

*

took company
mornings
drew pleasure around me

unfurled my new knot

forenoon, in haste

then saw
the red head
in splendid clothes

in the meadow,
afterwards the orchard

never offered
resistance

*

put on that coat of yours

fur
becalms the sea
unnaturally

saw
the elegant, wonderfully
equipped mistress
fittingly step out

pretty bird

saw her laugh
accustomed to
such linen

*

You can see
youth lacks wings

clothing cast off,
bodies kindled
arrogant, wanting death

*

hope & expectation
burn
with a moist damp fury

the snake
shakes off its vapor

on her
vaulting
adorned
wonderful
almost royal
ass

hang a cloak at once

some go by faith alone

not this one

*

O sinewy harp
let that hostile
& bitter country
boil and be
ineffectually
busy

CHAUCER MARGINALIA

PROLOGUE

once
practiced
whilom   guitar
haunteden   &
giternes   dice
overindulgence

dees
superfluitee   tore
after
rentee   dancing girls
tombesteres   with
shapely neat
Fetis   *smale*   pimps
bawdes
didn't know
luxure   *unkindely*   unnatural
niste   lechery

heeste   in full
command
dronkelewe   of
drunken
cursednesse!   wickedness
dampnacioun   &
damnation

141

hurried down
where
lies
amuse themselves

where
truly
light-hearted I
drew aside

upon my word
I itched

I dreamt also
in the devil's name
                          adoun / spedde;
            Ther
                  lith
                     hym / disporte and pleye,
                          drough   apart
                  ther

                               soothly
                                    light
                                         parfay
                     icched
               me mette eek
               a twenty devel wey!

142

at any rate innocence
always
benefits
from
box medicine

makes
fresh / malty
jokes

learns
decent
ribaldry

Algate   *sely*
                    alday
                            prow

    boiste   *letuarye* —

    doost
    moiste corny
    japes

        ribaudye
                lere

    honeste

it's sweet   *his*   *soote*
such liquid   *swich licour*

also   *eek*
grove & field   *holt and breathe*
shoots   *croppes*
eye   *yë —*
them   *hem*

                        daintee   fine
                        rood   road
            Ginglen   *pace*   jingles
                                                        pass away

      heeld   the same
            been   that
        til   are
        thilke   held
What   *wood*   to:
        swinke

        priking
            lust,
                purfiled

            grettere

144

balled,
steepe
souple   estat—
     forpined

palfrey

why it's crazy
to work

riding
pleasures
fur-lined
on a
great
bald
rib-protruding
wasted away
saddle horse
in
supple condition

campaigned
assembly of forces
thrice / always
the
same
against
reputation
& a
demeanor
of
rudeness

true / perfect

horses
wearing
thick cloth

curly
&
moderate

agile

great

reised
armee
thries   ay
ilke

again   pris

post

vilainye

verray, parfit

hors
fustion   wered

crulle

evene

delivere   greet

146

                    lady   to the
      Embrouded   lady's
                          rede   embroidered
            floiting,   red
                    endite   whistling
                    portraye   compose verse
      hote   sketched
            lowely,   hotly
                                  namo   humble
            arwes

                                                         no more
                                                          arrows

            bar / thriftily;   bear properly

        dresse   takel   gear toward
      not-heed   the
                                                    close-cut head

                    coude   know
                    swerd   the
                                                          sword

                          sheene   the
      Harneised   bright
            forster   mounted
                    soothly   forester
      Cleped   truly
      soong

147

Entuned   *fetisly*   named
                                                                    Elegance
                                                                    sang
                                                                    &
                                                                    chanted
                                                                    elegantly

moderate
nourishment
on   *mesurable*
blood-red, blue   *norissing*
                sanguin   *pers*
silk
                                   sendal

a pity   *scathe*

because   *For*
practice   *haunt*
surpassed
                passed
angry   *wrothe*
texture   *ground*

those   *dorste*
dared weighed
                                   weren
were
                                       reed
red
but
                                       moiste
unworn

even   *straunge*
foreigners   *coude*
knew

a
gap-toothed   *Gat-toothed*
veiled   *Ywimpled*
riding skirt   *foot-mantel*
spurs   *spores*
talk   *carpe:*

                        plein

                                                    one
            boomly   entirely
                                             unpretentious
                            dayesye   daisy
                                                      of
    delit   sensual delight won't
                                                     fill
                        plein   wine stocks
                                                    with
    envined   plenteous
                                                   snow
                        plentevous

snewed

149

THE WIFE OF BATH

Al

    fir

       freletee

          although
          frailty
          fires
          the
          spirit
          of

bigamye

    gost

          remarriage

tree

          wood
          ordains
  shifte
          the
welle,
          source
   parfitly —
          perfectly

          the
conclusioun
          end
Glose
          interprets
office
          excretion

innocent
equipment
of
virgins
be called
refined
stand-offish

sole
owner
of
morning

slave
of
purport entirely

sely
harneis

maide

pured
bote precious

daungerouse

morwe
dettour thral
sentence · *everydeel*

                                                    slender
                                          flirtatiousness
                                              everywhere

                                                    desires
                                                        by
                          daliaunce   leaking
                            smale —   mates
                          oval
                                                        by
        Coveiteth   villain
                                                    horses
                                                    possessed

                    chepe
            make

                            weelde
        dropping
                    shrewe!
            hors

                            152

singe
sleek
clothing

guard
your   *senge*
body
dear   *slik*
                                          borel
shorten
innocent   *wardecors*
barren   *keepe*
burns
                        leve   *shorte*
enjoy   *sely*
bound   *bareine*
suffering   *brenneth*

whinny   *shende*
                                          bonde
complain if   *pine!*
ruined

                                          whine

                        plaine and

                                          spilt

ba

kiss
patient
pudendum

suffrable
queinte

altogether
curse
taste
of

everydeel

shrewe

toothe

ferthe

paramour—

ragerye,

the fourth
mistress:
wantoness

untamable magpie
gracefully
deprived

Stibourne   pie:

smale

berafte

because
it
must
serve
the
greedy lecherous
bible's
good
poison
&
strive
for
husks

For

moste

siker

likerous

likerous

vinolent

boote

154

left
confidante   *laft*
secrets   *gossib*   *privetee*
    Bet   *thee*

better thrive   *biwrayed* *conseil*
on
disclosed secrets   *hire*

her   *everydeel*
entirely   *reed*   *hoot*
red / hot   *grace*
luck   *shapen*   *gites —*
destined   *frete*
dress   *daliaunce*
ate
flirtation

    sterte

    mette   runs
    upright   the
    dream
    supine
    dames lore

weep algate   mother's teaching
    wept anyhow

moten

usage   must custom

   purveyed   *make*   provide the mate

                  undertake   guarantee

                   bold   possession

                                believe

    trowe   the

                              gap-toothed

Gat-toothed   *wel-bigoon*   well-situated

                 likerousnesse   lecher

ever
sure salvation

ever
the
nice property
of
splendor

pleasure's
ear
grown
stubborn

stories
of
summer's
knowledge
strictly
roam
with
willow sticks

ay

wis   *savacioun*

hende
solempnitee
fee

list
list
weex

Stibourne

geestes

someres
witing   *faste*
roule
salwes

157

                                                        accustomed
            using   to
                                                          perverse
            wikked   casts
            cast
      weene,   *pine?*   thinking
                           fine   suffering
                                                             ends
                  wood   with
                          heed   raging
                                                             head
                  swough braide:
                                                    swoon started
                  mordred
deed   murdered
                                                           the
                        wite   dead
eftsoones
                            wreke   blamed
                                                          again
                                                            the
                  bridel   avenged
            brenne   bridle
                                                           burn
      maistrye   *sovereinetee*   or
                                                           skill
            lust   in the dominion
                                                            of
                                                       pleasure

158

deprived of
rape
petitioning

perhaps
chose
bone
guarantee

learned
satisfactory
sighs
provide
wantoness

rafte
oppression
pursuite

Paraventure
chese

suretee
boon

lere
suffisant

siketh
purveye
joliness

kike for
holden

biwraye

rake-stele

hele

vice

wiste
disfigure

dyde
conseil

swal

faste

"Biwray   soun,"
                  namo

kicked because
considered

disclosed
the
rakes's handle
concealed
defects

knew
deformity

160

                                         would die
                                            secret
                                               &
                                          swollen

                                           closed

                                  betraying sound
                                      to no one

                                         sentence;

                      selde
                   Prowesse

the topic   *beer*
is   *shette*   *thenne*
seldom
excellence   *brenne*

shut   *His*
the bear   *genterye*
thence

                            161

burn
its
gentility

annexed

kinde

boren

deed

its
related
nature
born
dead

renomee

bountee

straunge
poverte

drede

renown
magnanimity
alien poverty
&
doubt

             liking   pleasure:
             ouche   the
                                                       lecherous
likerous   trinket

for   that
                                                      constantly

        algates   dear
  leve

        cors   upright   imagines
                      bithinke   the
                                                     corpse supine

yCANTOS

&
the sun is
after that hour
floating
in
flame,
dry flame,
petal in wind. Ho!
& the old man
sweeping
the shore/Quiet
altered

I

And then
set
we
before sheep
heavy with wind
and
Weeping
Onward Belly
Circles
we
stretch
Sun

comes, then we
cover us
with mist
and
glitter
Stars
and
glue
Then prayed
for sacrifice
as
well
and
dark blood flowed
out of our youth

IA

Many
Men
Battle
these days
Pallor
slaughtered
poured
unto
Pluto
&

unsheathed
til I should bear
the
unburied
o
peaceful
spirit
Shattered
Facing
the
flood

II

Hang it
there
Sordello
but
lower
Sleek
under
the
eye
of the
Emperor
Move
back
among

Evils
and
ills
and doom
Let her
lithe
glass
slide
and the
sands
stretch
And
nipples
play
between my
fingers
So

II A

Come
spread
your
wet
and let
the red
rocks

glow
And ship
out
mad &
off her
course
Sleight
ivy
upon
her
&
Grape

IIB

awake
where
tendrils
heavy
out of nothing
break
the
hot
shadow
&
hot
sky

Lean
if you will
Rose
over my
face
and
allow
me
breath
Allow the
glass
grey
olive
&
smoked
salmon

III

bear
in
mind
I
sat
for her
there
Crossed
&

uncrossed
my
leg
Turned
from
the
apple
in
the
little
gallery
without
clothes
on
My silk
in
tatters
upon
the
ground

IV

the silver
down
beats
the
heart

and
black
crescent
curved
under
And she
went toward
the
window
where
my
heart
lay
in
a
dish
the
thick valley
lifting,

IVA

Thus
shallow / the
torches / is
blue
saffron

one scarlet
is
not a ray
bathing
me
This wind
Hay/shaking
Let
the
smoke hang
Guilt
be
gray

V

Great
Ecbatan
the bride
city
rushing
from
the
North
barren
old men
light

with souls
the fire
topaz
I
imagine
and fading

Vᴀ

And many
of thee
talks in the night
air full of women
lust
of night
song
or
land
And
he kept
a
dark
bath
&
steeped
in
slander
Hot

V B

The lake
and all
cast
in
all who
held
in
death
in
this
weather
smothered
in down
for the gossip
Burner
of
talk
rummy
sayings

VI

We knew
that
the stone
would be

wed
have
a son
would be thick
living
in the hand
that had known her
without issue

revert
to stone
Turning
by river-marsh

VIA

Need
not
wed
but
Eleanor
turning
thirty
My lady
Nor watch
fish
nor

fly
but find
song
that free
her

VII

Eleanor.
And then
the
phantom
marble
candles
file
before
us
Voices
under
fresh
marble
Discreet
suggestion
touched
with
thick
lipstick

Drinking

VIIA

Damn
Flimsy
in
our
things
&
under
petticoats
Silk
against skin
where
the sea
runs
Eleanor!

VIIB

Lamplight
at
daybreak
and
the cold

bit
her
skin
her nipples
that
had been
like
large eyes
tightened
with
wind

VIIc

And
the young
lie
in my arms
But Eros
lift up
the
stiff
The long
slender
slit
and
drift/under

VIII

These fragments
slang
that
river
of
received
matter

arranging peace
between
you

awaken
the/pubescent
summer
with
her

spread
the
sheets
with
wind

IX

One year rose
one year snows
one year hail
broken walls
in the hold
one year
water to neck
&
night
set up
speaking
its
mind

XV

Keep your
prayer
Holding it
hardened

inch by inch
The head rose
held downward
The face only

tongues
the top
into hardness
Holding the
Oblivion
how long!

And shield me
The gate swung
Panting
Bathed in
sunlight
Swollen

XVI

And before hell
dries
completely
& we
go running from
one another
plainly
slowly
sorely
screwing one another
w/out

perceptible moisture
naked
our heads held
back
to
the
flames

XVIA

And I bathed myself
of the hell
fallen
lake
of limbs
here an
embryo

Then light
the blue
grass
passage
and I
entered
the light
The plain
rising
in the quiet

Typeset at NewComp Graphics Center, a part of
Beyond Baroque Foundation, partially funded by the
National Endowment for the Arts.